*Only Golfers Can Understand*

MICHAEL PARDY

© Michael Pardy 2025

All rights reserved.

This book is copyright. Except for private study, research, criticism, or review no portion of this book may be reproduced without written permission from the publisher.

East Coast Australia Tour Edition, September 2025.
Florida, USA Tour Edition, October 2025

For all enquiries email: golfdogbook@gmail.com

Book Design: Nada Backovic
Illustrations: Matt Broughton

ISBN 9780987179371

*12 2 11 3 10 4 9 5 8 6 7*

# Table of Contents

Foreword ................................................................ 7
Our Friendship Runs ........................................ 11
What Is God? .................................................... 12
Up in the Air ..................................................... 13
Better Aiming ................................................... 14
Fast Track Golfers ........................................... 16
Full Grown Humans ......................................... 17
Dream Holes .................................................... 18
Careering ......................................................... 20
Romancing the Putt ......................................... 21
Good Golf ......................................................... 23
Slice ................................................................. 29
No One is Safe ................................................. 30
Bunker to Bunker ............................................. 31
Setting Boundaries .......................................... 32
Checkmate ....................................................... 35
No Redemption ................................................ 36
Tight Kerning ................................................... 37
I Meant to Say Delusory .................................. 38
William and the Golf Game .............................. 39
Recursive Compounding® .............................. 40

| | |
|---|---|
| How it Goes | 43 |
| Fyodor's Caddie | 44 |
| The Games We Play | 53 |
| How to Play Bunkers | 54 |
| Macaroons | 56 |
| Three Mantras | 57 |
| Perfect Practice | 58 |
| Poor Old Tiger | 60 |
| Live and Let Die | 61 |
| Getting Down with James Brown | 63 |
| Not a Metaphor For | 64 |
| Appendix A: Perfect Practice | 67 |
| Notes | 73 |
| Index | 77 |
| Acknowledgments | 79 |

*For Janet Paterson*

# Foreword

My plan was to study piano and practice chords and scales in the spare time between writing one poem and the next. I found a talented Scottish piano teacher and attended class once a week.

Each week in our friendly preamble to the lesson, my teacher would talk about his recent golf games and eventually we organized to meet at a nearby course.

Golf took over. I loved it so much that I neglected my writing and the piano.

To address the problem I pivoted to writing poems about golf and playing golf with my piano teacher.

This book is devoted to enjoying the ups and downs of the game. It is the perfect gift for anyone starting out, still going, or thinking about letting bygones be bygones and coming back home.

Thinking and laughing about golf is a surefire way to improve your game.

*Michael Pardy*, 2025

*"The least thing upset him on the links. He missed short putts because of the uproar of the butterflies in the adjoining meadows."*
—P.G. Wodehouse

*"I didn't miss the putt. I made the putt. The ball missed the hole."*
—Peter Jacobsen

*"Golf is a day spent in a round of strenuous idleness."*
—William Wordsworth

Shooter McGavin:
*"Just stay out of my way... or you'll pay! LISTEN to what I say!"*

Happy Gilmore:
*"Hey, why don't I just go eat some hay, make things out of clay, lay by the bay? I just may!"*

# Part 1

*In which we fall in love
and find there is nothing
more special than us*

# Our Friendship Runs

She's a golf ball, and I'm a putter,
I watch her dive into the cup,
If I was bread she'd be my butter.

My five wood warns to get a pre-nup
In case she runs off with Big Bertha
But I don't think we'll ever split up.

Our friendship runs and runs on further,
The way she rolls—so level and true,
Let's raise a toast to my flat earther:

    To my Spalding Hot Dot Number 2,
    There's never been a ball like you.

# What Is God?

What is God, if not a golf ball in flight?
Lofting into blue sky like it should,
Running true, straight on, and out of sight.

The holy spirit waits in golfer's blade
To turn a savage hook into a draw,
A rabid slice into a gentle fade.

Jesus, then, is a forgiving wood,
Come down from the nailing cross we made,
To bless us all with extra shots of good.

But what is golf? What is this great game for?
It's for all us dapper chaps to adore.

# Up in the Air

How far back my backswing swings
Behind my ear up high!
Oh, I do think it the pleasantest thing
To swing my ball to the sky.

Up in the air and onto the green
Where the flag waits by its side,
My ball sits in the prettiest scene
In all the countryside.

At the dog-leg left—the ball I send
Must jump the trees in a bound,
Up in the air it goes flying again,
Up in the air and around!

# Better Aiming

From Fyodor Dogski, 'Always On', Substack, 2025

In your car, whenever parking, especially at the golf course, take some extra time to make sure you are dead center and perfectly parallel to the white lines.

Although having a good aim comes naturally, a lack of trust can turn you crooked. Seek out every opportunity to keep your aim alive.

At the local fete have a go at Knock 'em Downs. Win a koala bear. If you have stationary crows on your telegraph wires, find some unripe apricots and put those crows on the move. At your local pub play a game of darts. On your way home walk straight. Do not sway. Write on unlined paper—exactly fifty lines on each page. If the lines go on a slant—your natural aim is off kilter. Uphill often means you hook, downhill—you slice. Concentrate on writing straighter and your drive will follow too.

A session of target shooting may also pay dividends but do not waste time with clay pigeons. Golf has no moving targets. There is little difference between lawn bowls and indoor carpet bowls; for our purposes they are both equally as good.

You might consider turning your hand to decorative sewing or tapestry. Being a good aim is useful for everything in life. Hanging pictures. Building a fence.

Good aim comes naturally. Sleeping babies are born with it—their eyelids seal in perfect semi-circles.

It's also how a hand finds a matchbox beside the bed and lights a smoke in the dark.

# Fast Track Golfers

Fast track golfers squashed inside motor carts,
Stuck high up on the ridge to wait their turn,
Fume over the slow play of two old farts.

The pair below amble without concern,
Two brothers with a mission to savor
Their ribbing and laughs at every turn.

They sip on beer and enjoy its flavor,
Their golfing prowess is beyond besmirch,
They show no fear and give no favor.

For too quick comes the day to fall from perch
Into a shiny box in a gloomy church.

# Full Grown Humans

Full grown humans ride their bikes in straight lines
Between road edge and heaving metal car.
But these days I prefer to split two nines

With a snack and a sip at clubhouse bar,
To study the index on my score card
To find a friendly hole, and one more par.

Ah Yes, I once rode bikes in lycra garb
With plastic bottles, and pink gels to suck,
But it's a sport I've come to disregard

Since in the reverb of a ball well struck
I heard the gasp of a superb fuck.

# Dream Holes

Precis of: Fyodor Dogski, 1999. 'Golfing and the Third Eye', All of Volume 2

Before you nod off, recall your favorite first hole and play it in your mind. The air is crisp and the sky is blue and your tee shot sails far away toward the oak tree. As you approach, see your bright white ball sitting high on the mown grass in the shade of the oak's grand canopy. Now notice that further in, closer to the trunk, Daisy—your clairvoyant caddie has unraveled a foldable short-legged drinks tray and prepared a single gin and tonic. On ice. For you. Take a sip and imagine your second shot. Take the shot. See it fly over the fairway bunker onto the bank at the back of the green. Take another sip and look up to notice your ball has turned itself toward the flag. Now you make a firm putt that sends your ball to within an inch of the hole; you tap it in with one hand for a par.

Move onto the next. Don't walk there. Just arrive. Dreams don't need walking. See the fairway in front of you. It's a par 3 of 150 yards. Across a valley. There's a slight headwind. Take an eight iron and send your ball flying high. See it land with a skip and hop in the middle of the green. Sink the putt for a birdie. Remind yourself that this has all already happened. You are dreaming your life. A par, another par, another birdie. Your life is all threes and fours and fives. It's the natural order. Even when you shank one, it hits a tree and bounces back into the middle. Fluff your pillow. You have all night. Morning can wait.

# Careering

What is this game you gave up golf for?
Away from rolling dunes and cellar door
Are there any rules? Do you keep a score?

What draws you to the morning traffic jam?
Egg McMuffin and one more kilogram?
Urgent Zoom calls on your dash-board phone cam?

In office blocks there are no mown fairways;
There's PowerPoint and cupcake share days
And anxious people, having bad hair days.

Your bills still bob about on rapid flows,
Careering in and out as your lifestyle grows
And time runs down the drain. Yes, there it goes.

What is this game, you gave up golf for?
Away from rolling dunes and cellar door
Are there any rules? Do you keep a score?

# Romancing the Putt

From Fyodor Dogski, 1968. *Beginning Golf*,
Vol. 9 Chapter XVI, pp 1163-1164.

A golf ball will fall when most of the ball rolls over the air. The air is the see-through circle that has no grass on top. If half the ball is rolling on the air and the other half is rolling on the grass—the ball will not fall. Furthermore, if the ball is travelling too fast it will also not fall—even when all of the ball is rolling over the air. The ball might toy with you, dip in and out, but it won't stay long. Ninety percent of balls travelling at the speed of 3 feet past the hole will resist gravity. Have you ever seen a ball with an up-turned nose do a daredevil loop around the cup before popping out the side door? Of course you have.

Some balls are more petulant than others. If you discover a petulant ball in your kit, hit it far into the distance or into a lake, if there's one handy. If you happen to chance upon your outcast ball sitting proud on the side of a fairway, looking all innocent—blank it! Life is short.

With a good ball the surest way to have fewer putts is to use your charm. When it's treated right, a good ball will fall in love with gravity.

For example, on the green always pick up your ball and polish it tenderly. Whisper in its ear: "Don't tell anyone... but this hole is my summer residence. You can drop by anytime. We can play scrabble or listen to records. I have a coffee machine. Even when I'm not here you can go inside and make yourself at home. I'll show you where the key is."

# Good Golf

How does it feel?
It feels
Like a click,
The sound of a click.
Feel the click
Midway through the swing,
Through the arc,
Your body turning,
All of it in a circle
Where the ball connects
There's no bump,
No resist,
Just a click.
Good golf feels like that click.
It feels lively,
All of it lively,
Your feet on the ground,
Energy flows up
Through your heels,
Your arches,
Your balls,

Your toes.
The energy flows
And you step lightly.
The ground is rubber,
The energy springs
Up your legs,
Through your trunk,
Your chest,
Your back,
Your shoulders,
Your neck,
Out your eyes
Into the air.
Good golf feels like your soul
Is flying inside the ball.
In the air and the sky,
Over hills and sand,
Over green and blue
Into the surroundings,
Surrounding the surrounds.
Surrounding the sounds,
Surrounding all the people,
Who click and swoosh

And spin and move,
Who smile and laugh.
Good golf feels like an extra dance step,
Stepping out of the rhythm
In between two beats,
Turning towards
A gap through a door
To a view of a scene
No-one's seen before
On the green for the last dance,
Good golf feels like
Everything has slowed.
Time rolls smooth
The world tips,
And all that is in it
Trickles singular,
Dropping into the hole
Flowing out to sea.

# Part 2

*In which the honeymoon ends
and missed putts and wayward
drives require counselling*

# Slice

I'm estranged from my children and wife;
Even my beloved golf is down the drain.
I must confess—I'm failing at life.

It's all my fault, there's only me to blame,
But I'm sure everything will soon improve,
If I can take that slice out of my game.

If that flaw in myself I can remove,
The shadow will lift, and the sun will rise,
Next time we play you might say: Dude,

You've changed. There's a sparkle in your eyes
And your ball goes as straight as arrow flies.

## No One is Safe

You will never be safe, until the ball

    It falls without a trace

        To its final resting place

           And calm returns to your face.

# Bunker to Bunker

Your second shot is the one to perfect:
It stops things going from bad to worse;
It helps you end better than you expect.

A half full glass will still reduce your thirst,
And with fewer drinks you'll get less drunker;
You might even jump from last to first.

That said, do not dare play Casablanca;
It's where the woods all lead into the mire
And every bunker throws to deeper bunker.

At Casablanca, you slide from fry pan onto pyre,
And that smell… well, it's your pants, they're on fire.

# Setting Boundaries

From a lecture given by the author in the Grand Ballroom at Fyodor Dogski Institute last year.

"Give it a real hoick," says the little man on my shoulder. Out of the corner of my eye I see my clubhead bolting away past my ear then swinging sharply around the back of my head nearly hitting me in the nose. I hit the brakes, flinch and grunt and swing back hard with a huge haymaker. My club thumps the ground and dropkicks the ball, sending it racing like a scolded cat: bumping, tumbling, and diving deep into the thorny bush beside the ladies tee. My heart sinks. That ball cost nine dollars. Lost first shot.

My little man had good intentions. In this case he wanted to impress the group waiting to go next. He wanted them to know they were waiting behind a player who can drive it 250 yards. He remembers that one magical shot from the summer of sixteen. He can still hear the sound of it. Give it a hoick.

Don't get me wrong—I like my little man. He loves a good time. He often says things like: "Go on, just have one more." Or: "Let's ask her. She looks like she wants to dance." Or (just yesterday): "You really do deserve a convertible—at least for the summer."

But because of his untimely comments on the golf course, I have now instituted strict access limits. Before I address the ball my little man must go and stand behind the rope and bite his tongue. Only my inner golfer is permitted into the playing zone. It's not just the little man who is banished. The coach in me, the parent in me, the friend in me, the student in me... all the different me's in me must go and stand behind the rope.

I bought some new tech from the pro-shop to help. It's an electronic button attached to the top of my golf bag. This simple gadget has already improved my score by six strokes. When I press the button it flashes amber and makes a whirring sound. It's the sound of a large invisible dome being lowered over me.

The button light on top of my bag changes from amber to bright green as soon as the dome is fully lowered. It's then I know I am safe inside my own world.

I've also got a Zap Cap that gives a micro shock and empties my mind of all swing thoughts. At that point the only thing inside my head is a blank page with the words: "This Page Intentionally Blank". I slow my breathing and watch the words dissolve one by one from left to right. Page Intentionally Blank. Intentionally Blank. Blank.

In true blankness my club swings in a perfect arc inside the dome and I watch the ball set sail. When my ball comes to rest, if you listen carefully you can hear the dome rise. I feel the cool breeze.

The results have been so good I'm starting to worry. How long will it last? Of course the little man is always first over with his congratulations and a suggestion on what we should do next.

Maybe that's why I'm worried. He was too quick to arrive this time. I suspect he's found a way to hide inside the dome.

I can't stop thinking about it.

# Checkmate

I feel as powerful as an ivory queen
On the practice range at dawn's first light
The sun's rays warming my pre-game routine.

But in the real game, a shank to the right
Goes deep into a field of weeping corn,
And I limp about—a wounded knight.

When I four putt, I become a puny pawn,
Whose early gleam is now but dread remorse;
I cast about, hoping for a Unicorn.

A golfer who can stick and stay the course
May ride back home on that rarest horse.

## No Redemption

The aim of the game is the lowest score.

The game is not speaking to something more important.

There is no hidden message.

The truth is:
    If you miss the putt
    Your chance is gone…
    Add one stroke on.

# Tight Kerning

I'll book in for the Wednesday after next,
At Bayview Heights. I'll get back with the time.
My coach sent me some special tips by text

But there's so many things to fill my mind:
Chicken-wing, back-swing; my brain needs space
So I've erased old words like *za* and *tine*.

Scrabble and crosswords have lost pride of place,
Good golfers all need roomy frontal lobes,
We must store our scores in 4 point lowercase.

At the Pro Shop, they sell caps with zap probes,
Which turn your skull into vacuum light globes.

# I Meant to Say Delusory

Golf is a mental game in your head
Piano is nearly as difficult
Except it is played on a polished floor

Twenty is not too old to retire
If you intend to break par
And play concert piano.

Poetry too, is pretty tricky—
Especially if you want to rhyme.
At the end you also need to make up a title.

When it comes to painting
I recommend starting first with
Red square on Black circle
And NOT the other way around.

It must also be noted that Jazz is for the illusory,
It's on every Saturday at 2 pm in Cup of Tea Alley.

# William and the Golf Game

When William Shakespeare took his turn to play,
His first drive did not pass the ladies tee,
His laments rang around the course all day:
Is it nobler to be, or not to bloody be?
Is this a dagger I see before a bard?
Is a shank still a shank by any other name?
How can a sand wedge stab and stab so hard?
Do I dare compare a season to this game?
Like a summer's day of slings and arrows?
Must we welcome mishits as good fortune?
Or praise the fates for oversize marrows?
Is this the last hole? Will the torment end soon?

    When William trips on Yorick's skull, hidden in the rough

    He throws his club and yells: *Puck golf, I've had enough*!

# Recursive Compounding®

Verbatim text from a brochure left on the windscreens of all cars parked at Yarra Bend Golf Course last Sunday.

Here is a secret you will forget immediately: The better you get—the better you get.

Did your mind just blank that?

When you question your mind it will say something like: I forgot because it is too obvious and a waste of memory cells. You have far more important things to remember. For instance, your trailing wrist must press into the space above your hip before you begin your backswing.

Our minds make up reasons for everything. That time your desk phone rang and you lifted your coffee cup to your ear—I pretended not to see. I'm sure you had an explanation but I didn't want to hear.

It's not that complicated. Forgetting is easily fixable. Forgetting is merely not remembering. Every important thing is still there inside you.

Today… many of us throw our thoughts onto one big pile. It makes it hard to find them again. It's the same with your photos.

For instance when I think:

Next time I'm at Aldi I'll get that hair gel in the tall blue jar. It goes on the pile.

Or: This week the trivia quiz is on Wednesday not Thursday. On the pile.

What do the letters in my spectrum stand for again? On the pile.

Here are three words to sprinkle over the pile: Remember to Remember.

Remember to remember: The straighter you hit the straighter you hit. The fewer putts the fewer putts. The more you trust the more you trust. The better you get the better you get. The more you love the more you love. The richer the richer…

The yield from Recursive Compounding is high. At a minimum you are guaranteed an early and enjoyable retirement as a scratch golfer.

If you invest early enough, you might end up turning pro.

Do you want to learn more?

The Fyodor Dogski Institute runs both online and face to face training for different industry verticals. Surgeons, Emergency Workers, and Track and Field stars are experiencing never-before-imagined results.

Our six week summer training course is now accepting applications, especially from golfers. The demand for Certified Trainers is exploding. After three years Certified Trainers are expected to earn high six figures.

Please go to recursivecompounding.info to register. Use the code GOFL25 for a 25% discount.

Offer ends at midnight.

# How it Goes

Chipping over the bunker is the plan
But my wrist spasms in a sudden seizure
My ball sputters out—onto wet, hard sand.

I breathe in deep like a yoga teacher
But I can't stop a glance out to my left
And there I go… into water feature.

At the last, a group watching from the deck
Cheer when I pitch the ball off gravelly ground
And salvage a par from the day's shipwreck.

Our foursome shakes hands and makes pleasant sounds
As we confirm a time for next week's round.

# Fyodor's Caddie

I took a posting to West Head in Flinders,
A commodore position to oversee
Ammunition exercises.
Always on Tuesdays, commencing at eleven a.m.
And sometimes for special events on Fridays.
Officers receive full membership to
Flinders Links Golf Course, squeezed between
The sea cliffs and dirt road to the store.
The club insists that for the first three games
New members be chaperoned
By one of the club caddies.
They assigned me a caddie dressed in a floppy
Sun hat and baggie tracks.
Her name was Daisy, but she asks me to call her
Caddie.
She comes and stands by my side wherever the
ball lands.
She searches forward,
Entranced by some small thing moving in the
distance.
She speaks staccato phrases:

Slight breeze from left.
One hundred eighty yards.
Five wood.
Mid green.
Straight at flag.
At first I swing hard as she talks
But I learn to listen and now wait until she steps back
Well away, to a spot from where she watches me
Manifest her vision as best I can.
Caddie agrees to stay on beyond the three games.
We change our time to Mondays at dawn
Alone in the sunrise and sea mist
My ball makes curved lines in the frost.
I imagine she can read those lines,
Understand me and see ways to lower my score.
On the 8th hole she whispers:
Take your long iron,
One club extra,
Your three not four,
Hit it fat with all your power,
Directly toward that bunker.

Hit the rake.
Yes hit the rake.
So I hit the rake and my ball ricochets
To within a foot of the hole.
The following week
On the exact day I first break 80,
The navy posts me to Brisbane.
But Flinders and Golf have me in their grip.
I resign and buy a lawn mowing business.
We continued to play on Mondays.
On the par 5 they call Siberia,
Caddie says:
Your tee shot now stutters at its apex.
Your new job is wrong for you.
You should stop.
Something else will come.
And so it happens. I buy a people mover
And take groups on winery tours.
My tee shot comes back longer and more direct.
I ask her to marry me.
She says no.

She says it is not possible for me
To be your caddie and also your wife.
When I press she cries and says
If I say yes,
By next April... on the 14th
You will attempt suicide;
You will miss by half a ball to the left.
I say, better you stay as my caddie.
She nods and marries a chef the following year.
He plays piano.
I attend the service.
She is wrapped in a long silver skirt.
Her right shoulder and arm are completely bare.
She shines like a porcelain doll.
I stop playing golf for a while.
We both move away.

She opens a restaurant in the city.
The wine tour market slows down.
I sometimes drive for Uber now.
In Collins St I look in the rear view
See her in my back seat.
She smiles but we don't speak.
When I drop her, she turns and asks for a receipt.
On the blank side she prints three letters,
Hands it back.
She speaks staccato phrases:
A very good stock.
Very soon.
Even today.
You must buy.

# Part 3

*In which we return to endless shorelines
and quietly make peace with
unattainable perfection*

# The Games We Play

On long weekends, we all play Stableford:
At each tee there is a brand-new day,
A bright sunrise cheering us on to good.

The annual medal is always Stroke Play
All nerves and tremors and falling dominoes
Flipping in with the wet, warm, sleepy cray.

On odd loose-end days, I play Ambrose
With just me and my imaginary twin,
Marching resplendent in identical clothes.

My favorite though, is Closest to the Pin
One god-like loft, is all it takes to win.

# How to Play Bunkers

Even when you're standing in one,
Never call a bunker by its name.

Bunkers rely on intimidation,
Their shell-grit eyes can pierce a nerve.

Never engage in a staring contest,
Even the shallowest bunkers won't look away.

Like a card player with a jittery bluff,
Bunkers are simply another tricky lie.

They're no more trouble than a large divot,
Or clasping fescue on the fairway edge.

To annoy a bunker—mention it is banned
From Saltleaf Preserve and that course in Yea.

By far, the best way to gain the upper hand,
Is to master the art of disappearing.

You must practice going in and out
Until you are gone before you have left.

Never let a bunker see you practice.
A bull sees the Matador but once.

Go to a beach where no one knows your name
Shake your towel and disappear from the sand.

Disguised as a gardener, also practice
Walking backwards—raking over your tracks.

## Macaroons

Over undulating sandy dunes,
Where flags and tiny holes are peppered,
Appear the ladies with the macaroons

To share morning tea with Alan Shepard,
The handsome golfing astronaut,
Who took two spots from a leopard

To the moon and swung the club he wrought,
To become the furthest earthly chap
To unburden us with weightless sport.

Without gravity, you get more snap
And those leopard spots—fly off the map.

# Three Mantras

As you walk to your ball it's good to look at the scenery and repeat a mantra. This takes up the space in your mind where swing thoughts often go. Below are three suggestions.

Go forward, stay in play, two putts
Go forward, stay in play, two putts
(Repeat)

For every shot, choose a spot, where the ball will go.
For every shot, choose a spot, where the ball will go.
(Repeat)

Trust your next shot, trust every shot, trust your next shot most
Trust your next shot, trust every shot, trust your next shot most
(Repeat)

Make up some mantras of your own.

# Perfect Practice

From Fyodor Dogski, 2016. *Beginning Golf*,
Vol. 2 Chapter IV, pp 126-131.

Go to your local golf club and play the same 3 or 4 holes in a loop. When a shot does not reach your target, pick up the ball and carry it to where you intended. Have your next shot from there.

Do it like this and you are practicing the shots a good player typically makes. Do it like this and you are not practicing recovery shots. You are not practicing third putts. You are not making bad shots more likely.

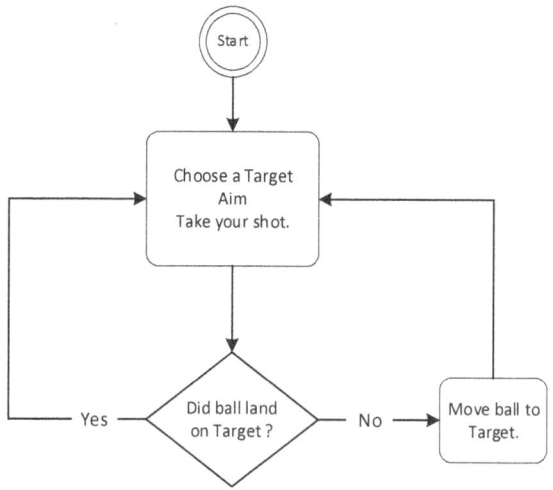

It's the same as how you keep going out with Joshua Burns and he ends up dragging you into trouble.

It's time to break away. Stop taking Josh to the golf course with you. Take him tenpin bowling instead.

For more details on Perfect Practice, see Appendix A at the end of this book.

# Poor Old Tiger

More than a dozen very pretty women
Claim to have lit Tiger Woods's wick
In five star rooms upon silky linen.

The daily rags filled with salacious pics:
Let's all slay the Tiger the headlines bayed;
In our circle—that man no longer fits.

The corporate sponsors said they felt betrayed,
And held back his money—to do what's right
For Tag Heuer, Gillette, and Gatorade.

Poor old Tiger had some worrisome nights,
But each dawn, he jogged on, in loyal Nikes.

# Live and Let Die

I watch him five putt, close up on unreadable
green.    Too firm, sail past, lip-out, bounce off,
inscrutable green.

He says it's the devil's game, where ten feet counts
the same,    As one teetering inch, on
unaccountable green.

When the owl at the kiosk says we're all out of
quince,    In the ball rinse—he finds the key to
runcible green.

He unlocks a deep dark door down to daring
dance floor,    And steps on silent tip-toe across
skateable green.

But the doom clouds still gather, god's furniture
rumbles,    And the lightening digs cracks on
combustible green.

In a nail-biting twist, his ball shies from a kiss,
The fearsome yips—tie up his wrists, on ineffable green.

Suave as Bond, he escapes over the edge of a cliff,
And with daring chip, he wins on invincible green.

As credits roll, Michael stands in gaudy plus fours,
Signing off scores—shaking hands on impeccable green.

# Getting Down with James Brown

Your effortless swing glides in silently,
Picks you up and takes you to funky town.
You're so loose, and you're so damn mindlessly

Golfing on your good foot, spinning around
Transmitting sonic missiles to the hole,
You're doing the shimmy with Mister James
Brown.

Get back, step light, let go, give up control;
Sit tight and let the clubhead smoothe its move;
Embrace the Dancing Wu Lees in your soul.

Some days are just too good to improve
So stay inside the pocket of the groove.

# Not a Metaphor For

*"life is golf in miniature."*
   —Stephen Potter, Golfmanship, 1968

ix

Life or chess dot com is a worthwhile
Way to whittle away the empty
Hours between one game and the next.
Or after a poor round you might turn
At last to painting that architrave
Around the small window that has sat
Waiting patiently for years to look
The same as every other window
In the house, but you know it's too late,

viii

A bridge too far. It's best to pretend
You first must attend to normal things:
Fit in, go for dinner, talk with friends,
Let golfish thoughts slip in now and then,
Especially out walking with your dog
Choking on his chain, swishing his tail,
Spalding Hot Dots winking right at you,
Making it obvious—like a smile.

vii
Now it's impossible to live life:
Have a car breakdown, visit a row
Of shops, attend a birthday party,
Wake up, catch a train, go to work—
Without sinking in, and drowning on
An overflowing palette of thoughts
About the latest Ping or your swing.

vi
Then when you squish some ants, you realize
This "impossible-life" is not much.
It's there in your browsing history
Or shopping trolley full of things,
Missed calls and dismissed reminders,
Which can all be rearranged anew.

v
On days when everything feels alright
Life mistakes itself for the main game
But life is an unsatisfying
Pastime shoved in between tee offs:
A day, a month, or ten years apart.

iv
Life is an often-used metaphor
For golf, but golf cannot say the same.
Golf is nothing at all like this life.
This life heads toward a dead end, but

iii
Golf follows along endless shore lines,
Linking eternal experience
To unattainable perfection.

ii
The new moon, it hankers to play golf,
To be a dimpled sphere in motion.

i
In your car boot, your clubs lie in wait.

# Appendix A: Perfect Practice

## How to Play

Perfect Practice follows the normal rules of golf except you pick up your ball when it does not reach your target and move it to its intended destination.

You can play Perfect Practice against yourself or someone else.

The winner of Perfect Practice is the player who moves their ball the least number of times.

## When to move your ball

You must move your ball if:

- Your ball does not reach your target area
- Your ball lands off the fairway
- Your ball lands in a bunker
- Your ball is obstructed and not subject to free relief under the rules of golf
- Your approach shot does not land on the green
- Your first putt finishes more than a putter length from the hole
- Your second putt misses

## Where to move your ball:

For an errant drive:

On a par 3 move your ball to the nearest edge of the green.

On a par 4 and par 5 move your ball to your first target.

For an errant second shot:

Not applicable for a par 3 (see Errant First and Second Putt below).

On a par 4 move your ball to the nearest edge of green.

On a par 5 move your ball to your second target.

For an errant third shot:

On a par 5 move your ball to the nearest edge of the green.

For an errant fourth shot:

There are no fourth shots in Perfect Practice.

For an errant first putt

If your first putt lands more than a yard from the hole move it to within a putter's length.

FOR AN ERRANT SECOND PUTT

Move your ball to the tee on the next hole. There are no third putts.

## How to score

Whenever you must move your ball the shot that missed receives 0 points.

PAR 3

1 point if your drive lands on the green.

1 point if your first putt stops within a putter length of the hole.

2 points if your first putt goes in the hole.

1 point if your second putt goes in the hole.

We do not practice third putts.

PAR 4

1 point if your drive lands on target.

1 point if your second shot lands on the green.

1 point if your first putt stops within a putter length of the hole.

2 points if your first putt goes in the hole.

1 point if your second putt goes in the hole.

PAR 5

1 point if your drive lands on target.

1 point if your second shot lands on target.

1 point if your third shot lands on target.

1 point if your first putt stops within a putter length of the hole.

2 points if your first putt goes in the hole.

1 point if your second putt goes in the hole.

## When is a ball on target?

For your tee shot and your second shot you do not need to land exactly on the spot. You have some leeway.

| Tee shot | Within 40 yards of your exact target and on the green for Par 3. |
| --- | --- |
| 2nd shot | Within 20 yards of your exact target and on the green for Par 4. |
| 3rd shot | Anywhere on the green for Par 5. |
| First putt | Within 1 putter length of the hole. |
| Second putt | In the hole. |

## Example Scorecard

| Hole | 1 | 2 | 3 | 4 | ... |
|---|---|---|---|---|---|
| Distance | 311 | 156 | 428 | 240 | |
| Par | 4 | 3 | 5 | 4 | |
| | | | | | |
| Tee Shot | 1 | 1 | 0 | 1 | |
| 2nd Shot | 0 | N/A | 1 | 1 | |
| 3rd Shot | N/A | N/A | 1 | N/A | |
| 1st Putt | 1 | 1 | 0 | 1 | |
| 2nd Putt | 1 | 0 | 1 | N/A | |
| Result | 3 | 2 | 3 | 4 | |

Hole 1: My first shot is on target. My second shot misses badly. I carry my ball to the edge of the green. My first putt goes close. My second putt drops. I score 3 good shots.

Hole 2: My tee shot lands on the green. There are no second or third shots on a Par 3. My first putt is less than a yard from the hole. I miss my second putt. I score 2 good shots.

Hole 3: My tee shot lands in the lake. I take a new ball and carry it to my target. My second shot lands close to where I was aiming. My third shot is on the green in regulation. My first putt is well short, so I move it to a putter length from the hole. My second putt drops. I score 3 good shots.

Hole 4: Tee shot is on target. My approach shot lands on the green. My first putt stops within a putter length. My second putt drops. I score 4 good shots.

## Extra

On those days where nothing works, grant yourself one or two mulligans. Everyone needs a little make-believe.

# Notes

*Our Friendship Runs*

This poem follows a pattern used frequently in this book. The pattern comprises 11 lines made from three rhyming interlocked tercets and a final couplet.

Spalding began making golf balls in 1897. The Hot Dot was called "the ball of fire." The larger dimples take the ball further. Spalding also made barbells, dumbbells, punching bags, rowing machines, fencing blades, whistles, shot puts, javelins, golf clubs, and published sports books.

*Up in the Air*

Inspired by Robert Louis Stevenson's *The Swing*.

*Fyodor Dogski*

An invented persona whose golfing ideas draws heavily on the Large Language Model (LLM) located on an Apache Kafka node embedded in the poet's occipital lobe. Most of the data in the LLM is scraped from transcripts of golf videos on You Tube.

*Careering*

This poem is the golf version of *Harp Song of the Dane Women* by Rudyard Kipling 1906.

*No One is Safe*

Sometimes you are on the green for two and end up with a double bogey. No one is ever safe. This poem follows the Welsh poetic form called *the straight one-rhymed englyn*.

*Tight Kerning*

Electronic Dome Buttons are available to purchase from the author's Instagram shop. Leopard Spot golf balls are also on sale there.

*Checkmate*

In this poem, a *unicorn* is a momentous shot that stays in your memory (and sometimes you friend's memory) for ever. For example, chipping out of the rough into the cup from sixty yards.

*I Meant to Say Delusory*

Very specific advice is often the best kind to ignore. Cup of Tea Alley is not shown on any maps and has never existed.

*William and the Golf Game*

The poem uses the sonnet form. Note that the title may already be used for one of the Just William stories by Richmal Crompton.

*Fyodor's Caddie*

This poem came to me after reading "Farrell's Caddie", a short story by John Updike first published February 25 1991 in *The New Yorker* magazine. It also appears in Updike's collection of golf writings called *Golf Dreams*.

In the poem, the stock mentioned was WBT. It rises and falls like my golf scores.

*Macaroons*

On February 6, 1971, the astronaut Alan Shepard walked out onto the moon's surface and hit two golf balls into the distance using a 6 iron.

*Live and Let Die*

This poem uses the ghazal form.

I noticed that James Bond seemed to encounter all sorts of troubles but always won in the end. For a while I adopted Bond's style for my golf.

*Getting Down with James Brown*

It became very tiresome playing golf in the style of James Bond so I turned to James Brown and now concentrate on feeling the groove.

*Not a Metaphor For*

The Niner is a standard pattern in modern poetry. It contains 9 stanzas, each of 9 lines, and each line has 9 syllables. This poem is similar to the Niner except each stanza drops off a line until it fades away. I call this form a Fading Niner.

# Index

Alan Shepard, 56
ambrose, 53
arrow
    as straight as, 29
backswing, 13
ball
    hot dot, 11
    missing the hole, 8
    turning toward the
        hole, 19
bike riding, 17
birdie, 19
blank
    and life's shortness, 21
    in the mind, 40
    intentional, 34, 80
    side of receipt, 49
bread and butter, 11
bunker
    at Casablanca, 31
    chipping over, 43
    disappearing from, 55
    fairway, 18
    to bunker, 31
    versus divot, 54
caddie
    clairvoyant, 18

closest to the pin, 53
dapper chaps, 12
daredevil, 21
dogleg, 13
dreaming, 19
dunes
    sandy, 56
fluff your pillow, 19
friendship, 11
fry pan, 31
ghazal, 75
God
    and lofting, 53
    can't help, 36
    purpose of, 12
gofl, 42
gravity
    and Alan Shepard, 56
Happy Gilmore, 8
hole, 17
James Brown, 63
Jesus, 12
Joshua Burns, 59
Knock 'em Downs, 14
last to first, 31
leopard spots, 56
life

fail at, 29
lycra, 17
make-believe, 72
mindless, 63
mulligan, 72
Nike, 60
*P.G. Wodehouse*, 8
pawn
   in your cruel game, 35
pepper, 56
*Peter Jacobsen*, 8
Robert Louis
   Stevenson, 13
Rudyard Kipling, 74
runcible, 61
scrabble, 37
seizure, 43
shiny box, 16

slice, 29
slow play, 16
sonic missiles, 63
stableford, 53
stroke play, 53
superb gasp, 17
Tiger Woods, 60
tine, 37
turning pro, 41
unicorn, 35, 74
*William Wordsworth*, 8
wrist
   spasm, 43
   tied up, 62
   trailing, 40
Wu Lees, 63

# Acknowledgments

Everyone who reviewed the early versions of this book including Colin Thomson, Janet Paterson, John Waugh, Otto Leenstra, Norm Mallett, and Suzanne Spunner.

My golfing companions, especially: Portsea Nine Holers, Mark Abbott, Ian Gray, Paul and Kerry Rowson, Danny Bainbridge, David Clunn, John Sponner, David O'Regan, and my family.

My first ever golf coach Gavin Coyle, who reviewed and improved my swing and this book.

My colleagues at Mark Tredinnick's Poetry Studio, and the people who support live performance: Amy Campion, Siobhan Dooley, Laurence Hewson, Heather Forbes McKeon, and Julia Gardiner.

Special thanks to my piano teacher Neil Forring who steered me back toward my true calling.

This Page Intentionally Blank

Page Intentionally Blank

Intentionally Blank

Blank

www.ingramcontent.com/pod-product-compliance
Lightning Source LLC
Chambersburg PA
CBHW062104290426
44110CB00022B/2702